A tour through th...
island's mo...
symbolic landscap...

Formentera

Text : **Joan Montserrat**

Photography : **Melba Levick**

Jaume Serrat

Ricard Pla

▼ *TRIANGLE POSTALS*

"**-Formentera**!- *exclaimed Count Timaschef and Captain Servadac almost in unison.*"

The island sighted by these intrepid characters in "Journey Across the Solar System", one of **Jules Verne's** most interesting novels, bears little relation to the real Formentera, as they arrived at their destination by sledge, skating over a frozen seascape at a temperature of 22° below zero!

Visitors to the present-day Formentera also pronounce exclamations of delight on arrival, but the temperature is more benign and the water is among the best the Mediterranean can offer anywhere.

Open to the four cardinal points, these clean, refreshing waters wash the ample beaches and tiny, hidden coves that comprise the island's coastline. From **Ses Illetes** or **S'Alga** to **Es Caló**, from **Cala Saona** to the beaches of **Migjorn** or **Tramuntana**, everything is within easy and leisurely reach...one of the advantages of being such a little island. The old saying that favourably relates the smallness of the package to the quality of its contents may well have been coined with Formentera in mind.

The following images aim to evoke an overall impression of the island's many and diverse treasures.

The quiet island

A tiny enclave anchored in the Mediterranean sun, faithful to the traditions that a varied course of history has bestowed on it.

From La Savina to Es Caló

S'Espalmador and Es Trocadors

Traditional music and costumes
have pride of place in the local
festivities.

The quiet island

Formentera is the southern-most of the islands that form the **Comunitat Autònoma de Balears** and belongs, along with Eivissa and some other, minor, islets, to the sub-archi-pelago of the Pitiuses. The island measures less than 80 km2, and the climate is sub-arid. The prevalent vegetation is comprised of scrub, sabines and pines and the island's natural resources are limited to salt, cereals, herds of sheep and goats, a few vineyards and the cultivation of fig, almond and olive trees.

The Greek chronicler Strabon called the island **Ophiusa**,

land of reptiles, probably in reference to the inoffensive lizards whose colour changes in accordance with their surroundings. The bronze axes and discs (today housed in the Museu Arqueològic d'Eivissa i Formentera) along with recent discoveries of megalithic remains, confirm that the island was inhabited before 2000 BC. Other visitors were the Phoenicians, Carthaginians and the Romans (who named it **Frumentaria**, land of wheat) and exported local sun-dried figs to the capital of their empire.

During the last stages of the Muslim occupation of the Balearics, the population was virtually wiped out by a Norman expedition. The island was conquered by the kingdom of Catalunya and Aragón in 1235 but, in the 14th century, was uninhabited for a long period of time, during which it became an operational base for Turkish and Berber pirates. The most recent repopulation, which took place in 1697, was carried out by a group of Eivissan families.

Towards the end of the 1950s, the tourist revolution made its presence felt on the island, but growth and development has been less immoderate here than in the Balearics. This is due, not only to geographical limitations, but also to the type of tourists who first "discovered" the island. Coinciding with the beginning of the hippy movement, Formentera became the destination for young people from all over the world who found the unspoilt surroundings auspicious to the life-style they sought to follow. When this movement became more a fashion than a philosophy, many of its original devotees left the island for other locations. But the door to Formentera had been left ajar and soon, hotels and resorts were

making their appearance. It is within this framework that the tourist industry exists here today and, during the high season, the number of visitors triples that of the native population of about five thousand.

There is, however, a general-ized tendency to maintain a certain balance which is appar-ent, not only in the conservation of areas of natural interest, but also in the deep-rooted respect the *formenterencs* show for their cultural heritage.

The images that follow are of the present-day and show some aspects of the rural population, a very matriarchal society, which persists in age-old occupations and forms of dress. In the coun-tryside and, particularly, at any of the local *festes* visitors will have many opportunites to see this for themselves.

The principal festivity is the **Festa de Formentera**, which

takes place, in honour of St. Jaume, on July 25th, and is followed by Sta. Maria, the patron saint, on August 15th. In **La Savina** and **Es Pujols**, on July 16th, the festivities are of a markedly maritime nature in honour of the Verge del Carme, the patron of sailors. The *festes* of **Sant Ferran** take place on May 30th, those of **El Pilar** on October 12th, and, finally, those of **Sant Francesc** on December 3rd.

We would like to make one recommendation: although vehicles may be rented on the island and, if planned well in advance, it is possible to bring one's own, without doubt the best way to see the island is by bicycle. The distances on Formentera are such that nothing is beyond the reach of even the laziest cycler, and this form of transport offers the chance to see the island at its own, leisurely pace.

From La Savina to Es Caló

The port of **La Savina** is the gateway to Formentera. The harbour, whose size is in proportion to the rest of the island, must appear enormous to any *formenterenc* born less than thirty years ago. During this time it has evolved from being little more than a few moorages on the wall of the old fishing wharf, thanks to the construction of a harbour wall which has greatly increased both its capacity and safety. Today, it gives shelter to modern vessels from Eivissa, Sant Antoni or Santa

1. La Savina and the two estanys, *lakes*

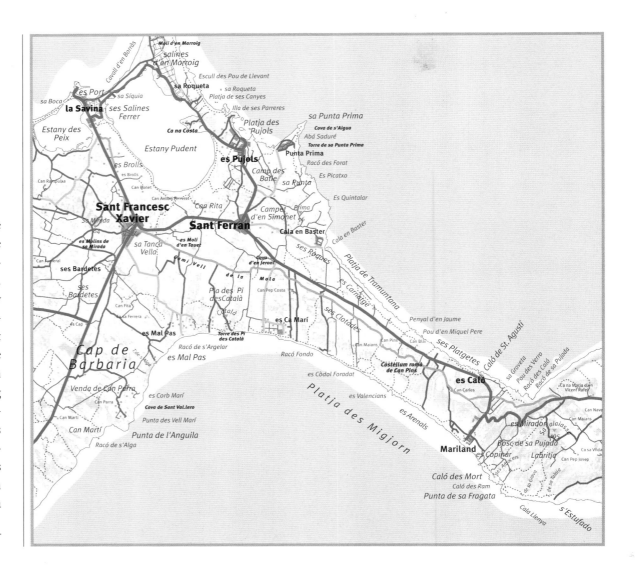

Eulària on the neighbouring island, and Alacant, Altea and Dènia on the Spanish mainland. The *Joven Dolores* or the *Illa de Formentera*, the old ferryboats from Eivissa, still offer the alternative of a slow crossing which gives plenty of time to tune in to the rhythm of the island.

In addition to these commercial passenger boats which bring residents, holidaymakers, and day-trippers to the island, many recreational craft also come to La Savina to take advantage of the modern facilities offered by the **Port Náutic**. Those of lesser draught can anchor in the nearby **Estany d'Es Peix** which, more than a lagoon, is a magnificent natural harbour which has access to the sea via a narrow mouth popularly known as **Sa Boca**.

The practical totality of La Savina has been taken over by new installations as a result of the

1

2

3

increased dimensions of the harbour, and there has been speculation about the possibility of reclaiming some of the non-productive salt pans. The majority of businesses are, logically, tourist-orientated and there are many restaurants who specialize in local, fresh fish.

A bird's-eye view of this area can only be perceived from the roof-tops as no natural view-point exists. The almost total lack of elevation above sea level would put the inhabitants in a precarious position should the waters turn against them. The monotony of the surrounding landscape is more than made up for by the spectacle provided by the limpid waters. It is worth spending several hours contemplating the changing effects of the sunlight on the **Estany d'Es**

1. *Landing on the island*
2. *Port Nàutic*
3. *A gourmet's dream*

Peix and **Estany Pudent** lakes, with their appearance of water-colour canvases, and the crystallized **Salines Ferrer** salt marshes. A leisurely stroll around the perimeter will enable us to appreciate the enormous ecological importance of this area. Both ornithologists and bird-watchers will enjoy observing the activities of the many and varied species of resident and migratory wildlife.

The greater of these lakes used to be known as the **Estany dels Flamencs** (flamingoes) when large numbers of these birds would gather here on their migratory routes, but today it is better known as the **Estany Pudent** (foul-smelling) due to the periodic putrefaction of organic residues. Between this lake and the sea, lie the **Salines d'en Marroig**, historically the

1 to 3. Still waters

1

2

most important saltworks. The installations themselves and the curious, gridded landscape they create form an interesting ensemble. The characteristic vegetation of areas of sand dunes comprises generally of sabines and tamarinds, but here, a few pine groves appear on the fringe of the saltpans.

Barely three kilometres separate the port of La Savina from the town of **Sant Francesc Xavier**. The old hamlet, which grew up in the shadow of a fortified church, is considered the island's capital by both native and adoptive *formenterencs*. At its heart, the aforementioned parish church, constructed in the early 18th century, doubles as a fortification, complete with powerful cannons, to defend the township against frequent pirate raids.

1 to 4. Views of the salt pans

1

Subsequently, the town hall was built, attached to the solid walls, and this main square is the scenario of the local *festes* in honour of the patron saint in December, as described in the prologue. No township is complete without a *festa* during the summer season, and to this purpose Sant Francesc has chosen to commemorate the Catalan conquest on August 8th.

Leaving the town on the road that leads to La Mola, after three kilometres we come to **Sant Ferran (de ses Roques)**, from where a turning towards the north will lead us to **Es Pujols**, the fourth township of this area. A study of these two geographical points, and the rural world which surrounds them at such close quarters along any of the unmade roads, would suffice to establish the sociological profile of the whole island.

1

Agreat part of the population, both natives and outsiders, live dispersed across the surrounding countryside and visit the townships for either commercial or recreational reasons. On market days and holidays, farmers, craftsmen and tourists all gather here. Visitors to the Fonda Pepe guest-house in **Sant Ferran** may feel they have entered a time-warp and returned to the heydays of the hippy movement of the sixties. Those tourists who seek sun, beaches and nightlife will find all their requirements fulfilled in the nearby holiday resort of **Es Pujols**.

Where as Sant Ferran's development was based on the exploitation of the salt-works industry, it is obvious that, in the case of **Es Pujols**,

1. *Main square, Sant Francesc Xavier*
2. *Ca na Costa and the Estany Pudent*
3. *Baptism by seawater*

tourism has been the motive force. The presence of the beach has attracted all kinds of establishments which serve the surrounding area, along with the resorts of **Sa Roqueta** and **Punta Prima**. This is the island's most developed resort centre and visitors will find all their needs catered for here. It would be a mistake, however, not to explore the rest of the island which has so much more to offer, and all within such easy reach, thanks to the shortness of the distances involved.

For example, the entire central part of the island can be explored in the course of a leisurely day's walking, whether it be along the main road, or, preferably, following the old

1. *Prickly pears*
2. *Meditating in the sun*
3. *Rural architecture*
4. *Es Pujols from Sa Punta Prima*

Camí Vell de la Mola and its many branches which lead to beaches both to the left and right. Taking **Sant Francesc**, or **Sant Ferran**, as our starting point (or **La Mola** if we travel in the reverse direction), an infinite number of walks which take us back and forth from the interior to the coast are at our disposal, each one with the added incentives of refreshing swims, the chance to chat in passing with a shephered tending his flock, or the sight of a Roman ruin such as the **Castellum de Can Pins**.

As for the discovery of the seaboard, not even the north coast presents any serious obstacles despite being somewhat more rugged than the south. Starting from the east, in **Sant Ferran**, and following

1. Es Pujols beach
2. Handicraft market
3 & 4. Beach scenes

2

3

4

fairly high escarpments, we arrive at **Cala en Baster**, the first point of interest, and traditional refuge for fishing boats. Beyond here, the cliffs lose height and form an extensive area of stony ground known as **Es Carnatge**.

Following this, we come to the **Platja de Tramuntana**, where the dominating north wind of the same name is responsible for a sparseness of sand which almost belies its denomination as a beach. Further ahead, the stretch of beaches known collectively as **Ses Platgetes**, which reaches as far as **Caló de Sant Agustí (Es Caló)** form an almost uninterrupted stretch of sand. This charming spot, where local fishermen have moored their boats since time immemorial,

1 & 2. Time stands still in rural inland Formentera

1

is the ideal place to stop for a rest and enjoy the view from one of the terraces.

Beyond here, the ancient **Camí de la Mola** begins its ascent, offering views on the way of the cliff faces which are studded with caves of considerable proportions. Discoveries here have proved that they have been used since prehistoric times as hideaways or dwelling places.

The south coast, between Mal Pas and Punta de sa Fragata, is one long expanse of sand, and this whole area is known collectively as **Platja des Migjorn**, although each sector has its own distinctive name. From the Es Pi d'es Català watchtower to the other, western extreme, we come across: **Es Ca Marí**, **Racó Fondo**, **Es**

1. Rustic dry docks, Cala en Baster
2 & 3. Caló de Sant Agustí

3

Còdol Foradat, Els Valencians, Els Arenals, Mariland... Some of these names indicate geographical features and ancient sources of water, but others are more recent and derive from the many resorts and establishments dotted along the coastline. There are so many bars and restaurants that there is no need to leave the beach in search of provisions. Behind the dunes, a narrow fringe of low vegetation forms the demarcation line between the two versants of the island.

Caló d'es Mort and **Caló d'es Ram** are the only rocky coves on this coastline and are situated at the extreme of the Platja d'Es Migjorn. Both are occupied by quaint old ramps used as dry docks and for launching fishing boats.

1 & 2. Es Migjorn beach, from Es Racó Fondo and Punta de Sa Fragata

1

They are more secluded than the nearby beaches, and are perfect sites for solitary sunbathing and swimming.

Here we come to the end of our visit to the narrow peninsula which forms the central sector of Formentera and whose peculiar geographical features make it such a characteristic part of the island. In few places is it so easy to contemplate at such close quarters the idyllic combination of inland, rural landscapes and the open sea.

1 & 3. Caló d'es Mort
2. Es Migjorn beach and Mariland

S'Espalmador & Es Trocadors

1

2

Any sailor arriving from the northeast who aims to make landfall in **La Savina**, must negotiate the reefs and shallow waters known here as **Ses Portes**. Already infamous in ancient times, they were mentioned by the Greeks in a mythical context. The widest of these straits lies between the Illa des Penjats, off the Eivissan coast and the **des Porcs** islet, from where the solitary lighthouse flashes a welcome, guiding beam to sailors.

This first islet precedes the larger **S'Espalmador** and beyond this, the long, narrow

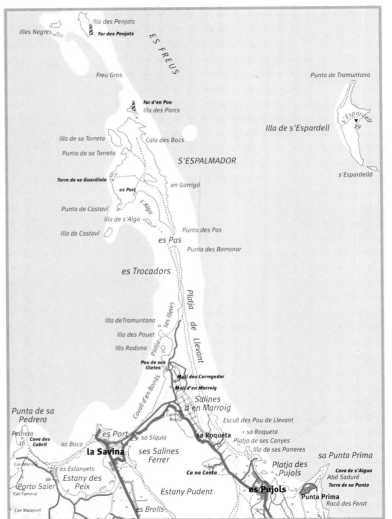

appendix that forms Formentera's northernmost extreme, the **Es Boronar** or **Es Trocadors** point. The second of these two names is the most frequently used but, in fact, should only be applied to the strait which separates the island and the islet, universally known as **Es Pas**. To the east of the two islets, at a distance of about three miles, yet another, **S'Espardell**, and, all around the ensemble, several other, smaller ones emerge from the surface of the water in fair weather.

This sector of the island's seaboard forms an intrinsic part of Formentera's character and its navegation tends to be an unforgettable experience, either in fair weather or foul, albeit for different reasons.

1 & 2. The sea, the only access route
3. The tip of the island with Eivissa in the background

The hinterland is best explored by bicycle and dressed for the beach, taking as starting point either **La Savina** or **Es Pujols** and travelling towards the north. Both routes take us close to the **Estany Pudent** and converge on the left bank of **Ses Salines**. If we leave from Es Pujols, we will cross, on the way, the inland peninsula of **Ca na Costa** where, recently, prehistoric remains of a megalithic tomb have been found.

The salt marshes (which have existed here since the Phoenicians but have now fallen into disuse) form, along with the Estany Pudent, a zone of great ecological importance. The size of this area, in proportion to the rest of the island, is very significant. Beyond the

1. *S'Espalmador*
2. *Illa des Porcs*
3. *Mud baths in S'Espalmador*
4. *Es Trucadors in the foreground*

1

2

3

4

saltern, the peninsula becomes so narrow that the two beaches, which lie on either side, almost touch back to back: to the east, the **Platja de Llevant** and to the west, **Ses Illetes**. Only a few sand dunes act as separation between them and bathers move at whim from one beach to another.

Despite their proximity, the two beaches vary greatly in appearance. Whereas Llevant is almost rectilinear, Ses Illetes is much more irregular and its name is derived from the five islets of various sizes which lie offshore. The **Molí d'es Carregador**, from where salt was handled and shipped to the mainland, still stands to the south. These beaches are very popular, partly because of the quality of the waters and, part-

1 & 3. *Molí d'es Carregador*
2 & 4. *Cavall d'en Borras beach*

1

2

3

ly due to the presence of a number of animated beach bars. Also, their disposition allows for sunbathing at any time of day and they have been established as nudist beaches now for years. At the same time, their proximity to La Savina brings them within easy reach of day trippers who arrive by boat.

Between the long peninsula and S'Espalmador, the sea barely covers the shallow marine floor which separates them. This strait, known as **Es Pas**, is easily crossed on foot if the sea is calm, which is usually the case during the summer months. In fact, crossing **Es Pas** has become almost a ritual, a kind of baptism or ratification among the island's many devotees. Whatever our motivation, however,

1 & 2. *Ses Illetes beach*
3. *Molí d'es Carregador*
4 & 5. *Time for a swim*

1

2

3

4

5

the splendid beach of **S'Alga** is reason enough to prompt us to attempt this singular excursion. Here we will see an old watchtower and a small marshland zone where cosmetic mud baths may be taken.

J ust off this western coast of the island, two historically important naval battles took place in the 15th and 16th centuries respectively. In 1529, the Admiral Rodrigo de Portuondo, lost great part of the Spanish imperial fleet to Red Beard's Turkish navy and, in 1651, Juan de Austria captured the "León Coronado", a privateer under the French flag.

1. *Llevant beach with S'Espardell in the background*
2. *Yachts sheltering in S'Alga*
3. *Crossing Es Pas on horseback*

Cap de Barbaria

The sector of the island which lies to the west of Sant Francesc is the quietest and most secluded, probably owing to the fact there is only one beach, **Cala Saona**.

The interest of this area lies in the many tracks and footpaths, unsuitable for vehicles but ideal for walking or cycling tours, which lead us to traditional old buildings and some pinewoods which unfortunately disappear as we travel southwards.

1 to 3. Cap de Barbaria, watchtower, lighthouse and general view

1

2

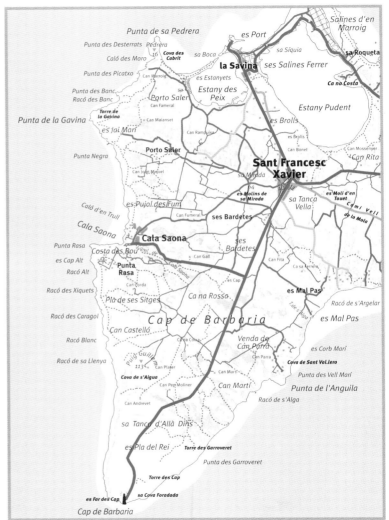

Punta de sa Pedrera · es Port · Salines d'en Marroig · Punta des Desterrats · Pedrera · Cova des Cabrit · sa Boca · sa Síquia · sa Roqueta · Caló des Moro · la Savina · ses Salines Ferrer · Punta des Picatxo · Can Marroig · es Estanyets · Ca na Costa · Punta des Banc · Porto Saler · Estany des Peix · Racó des Banc · Can Fameral · Torre de la Gavina · Can Maianset · es Brolls · Punta de la Gavina · es Jai Marí · Can Rampuixa · es Brolls · Can Bonet · Porto Saler · Can Mossenyer · Can Rita · Punta Negra · Can Joan Miquel · Sant Francesc Xavier · sa Mirada · es Molins de sa Mirada · es Molí d'en Tauet · Caló d'en Trull · es Pujol des Fum · Can Fumeral · sa Tanca Vella · Camí Vell de sa Mola · ses Bardetes · Cala Saona · ses Bardetes · Punta Rasa · Can Gall · Can Fita · Ca sa Ferrera · es Cap Alt · Costa des Bou · es Cap · Racó Alt · Punta Rasa · Can Corda · es Mal Pas · Racó des Xiquets · Ca na Rossa · Racó de s'Argelar · Racó des Caragol · Pla de ses Sitges · Cap de Barbaria · es Mal Pas · Racó Blanc · Can Castelló · Venda de Can Parra · es Corb Marí · Racó de sa Llenya · Puig Guillem 113 · Can Plater · Can Parra · Cova de Sant Val.lero · Cova de s'Aigua · Can Pep Moliner · Can Martí · Punta des Vell Marí · Can Martí · Punta de l'Anguila · Can Andrevet · Racó de s'Alga · sa Tanca d'Allà Dins · es Pla del Rei · Torre des Garroveret · Punta des Garroveret · Torre des Cap · es Far des Cap · sa Cova Foradada · Cap de Barbaria

From **Porto Saler**, a centre close to the Estany des Peix, a short walk leads us to **Punta de la Gavina** where an 18th century watchtower still stands. Both this headland and Sa Pedrera, further to the north, are perfect vantage points for watching the spectacle of the sea breaking over the rocks on stormy days, with the impressive silhouette of the Es Vedrá rock on the horizon.

Cala Saona is strategically situated at the only point of this straight coastline to afford any kind of shelter, and has a good, sandy beach surrounded by pinewoods. These conditions have given rise to a tourist resort which reaches as far as the nearby **Punta Rasa** and the beginning of the sector known as **Cap de Barbaria**. From this point on, the terrain begins to

1 & 2. Views of Cala Saona

gain height progressively and the hinterland is given over to agriculture and woodlands.

The Cap de Barbaria road ends at the lighthouse of the same name, which marks Formentera's meridional point. The environs are desolate and arid and only a few scrub bushes struggle to survive here in the inhospitable terrain. The views of the rest of the island, the immensity of the sea and the neighbouring watchtowers of **des Garroveret** and **des Cap**, act as counterpoint to this barren panorama.

During the return journey, we can follow some of the turnings that will lead us to the southeastern coast. In the area between **Racó de s'Alga** and **Es Mal Pas**, many new houses have been built.

1. Country house
2. The end of a day's fishing
3. Punta de Sa Pedrera with Es Vedrà

La Mola

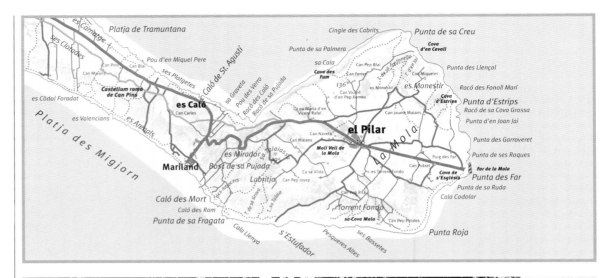

We have left La Mola until the end of our tour of Formentera as both its geographical position and its physical singularity set it apart from the rest of the island. Here, those visitors who have chosen to cycle around the island may, momentarily, regret their decision. The two kilometres of steep hill present a formidable challenge and the not so strenuous should consider the possibility of walking up ...or catching the bus.

1. The island from Es Mirador
2. La Mola

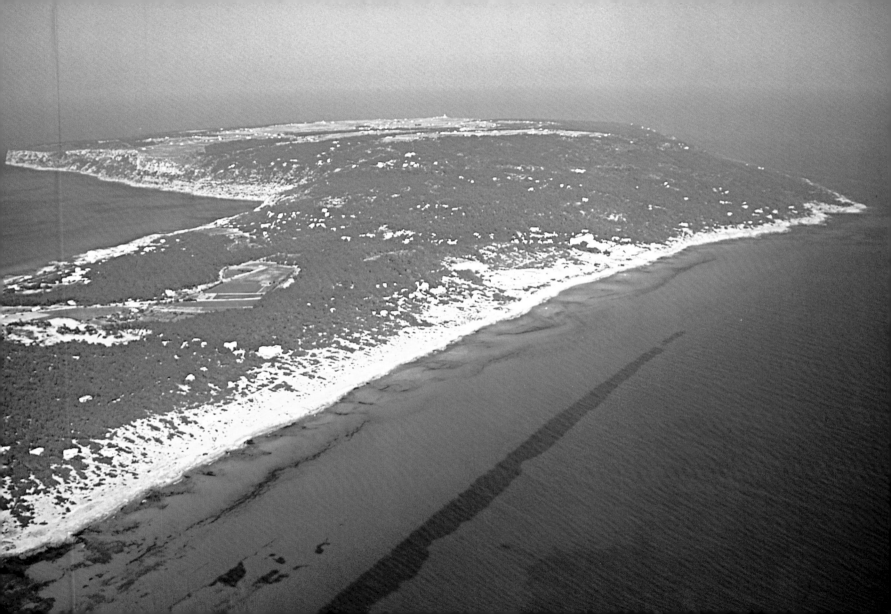

Whichever mode of transport is adopted, there is no doubt that the effort involved is more than compensated by what awaits us at the top.

This hillock, crowned by an ample plateau, has not only stood fast against the sea for millenia, but has also, in more recent times, defended itself in the face of the many changes that tourism has brought to the island, both to the landscape and to the people. Farming was once the only local activity, but artists and artisans established here today, have gone to great lengths to blend in with the environment. Proof of this can be found in the respect they show for the traditional architecture of the houses they have adapted to their needs.

1. The Tramuntana coast, from Es Caló to Punta Prima
2. Church of N^a S^a del Pilar
3 & 4. Rural architecture

2

3

4

1

2

3

The only nucleus of this area is the parish of **Nª Sª del Pilar**, whose tiny white church has become its symbol. Dotted across the rest of the plateau, there are numerous small constructions used for the storage of farm implements and other agricultural ends. Since the beginning of time, self-sufficiency has been vital for the islanders' survival and here, even now, cereals, vegetables and vines are cultivated with this goal in mind.

In order to fully appreciate La Mola as a whole, the visitor should take a walk along the paths which radiate from its centre. Those that lead southwards often take us, zigzagging, as far as the sea as the cliffs here are not very high.

1 & 2. Ripe and sun-dried figs
3 & 4. Old flour mill
5. Vines and prickly pears, elements of the rural garden

The path to **Sa Talaiassa** is particularly interesting as it takes us up to the highest point on the island. But perhaps the most authentic is the **Camí romà** or **des Frares**. The two alternative names, "Roman" or "of the friars", indicate that opinions are divided about its origins. It leads from **Es Caló** to the **Es Mirador** viewpoint, (some stretches still conserve the original cobblestones) passing, in continual ascent, through woodlands and offering splendid views along the way.

The **Far de Formentera** adds another twenty metres to the already impressive height of the cliffs which tower nearly one hundred and twenty metres above the sea. It was built during the reign of Queen

---

1. *The cliffs at Punta d'es Far*
2. *Geometrical plots on the La Mola plateau*

Isabel II, in 1861. A simple plaque, dedicated to **Jules Verne** has been placed near the lighthouse in gratitude for the mention of Formentera in one of his novels. The views from here are quite extraordinary and have served as inspiration to artists of all kinds.

The whole of the coastline to the north is characterized by the presence of numerous caves. At **Punta de Sa Creu**, one of the more rugged stretches, a custom born out of the necessity of the islanders' past was still practiced in recent times. Secured by ropes, they would climb down the cliff face to rob the nests of the *virots*, a kind of shearwaters who live in their hundreds in the cavities.

1 & 2. The La Mola lighthouse delimits the island

Traditions and festivities

In spite of the far-reaching changes brought about by the influence of tourism which have left their mark on many aspects of the island, the local people proudly maintain the ancestral custom of following the mode of dress of their peasant forefathers, whether it be when working on the land, when characteristic hats adorned with black ribbons are an essential, or when dressing up for a festivity.

1 & 4. Ancestral traditions and costumes are maintained in rural circles
2 & 3. Donning the emprendada *for a festivity*

2

3

4

In this latter case, the shawls, kerchiefs and aprons of the women are richly embroidered with thousands of flowers, and around the neck they wear the *emprendada*, the same traditional adornment worn for centuries

Music and dancing to the sound of typical local instruments such as the flute, tabor and large, engraved castanets accompany all the celebrations. *Ballades pageses*, or country dances, are very popular and also an ancestral game, *tirar al gall*, where the trophy is a live cockerel. Both these activities play an important role in traditional rituals of courtship among younger people. Visitors should not miss the chance to witness the beauty and authenticity of these *festes*, so emblematic of the island's character.

_____

1. *Traditional musical instruments*
2. Ballada pagesa *in Sant Francesc*

1

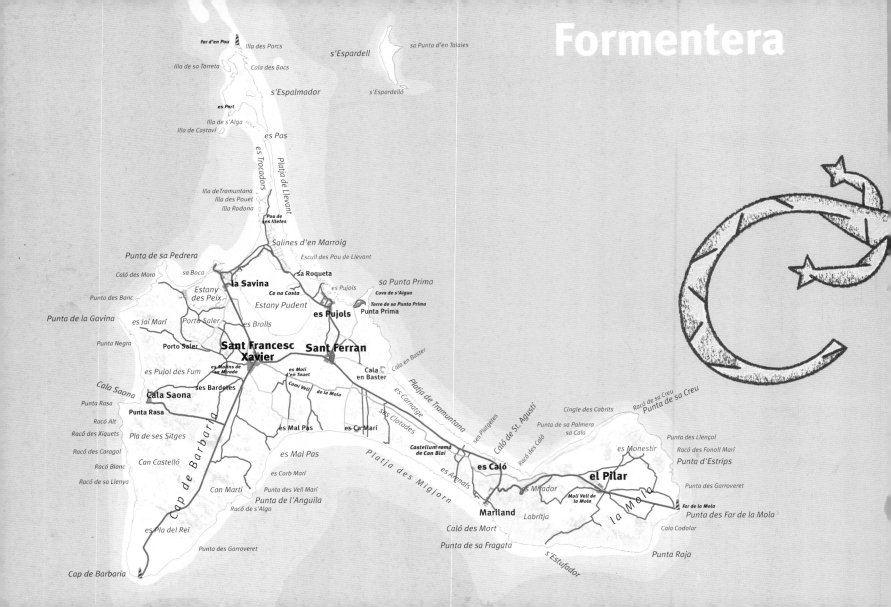

Formentera

Far d'en Pou
Illa des Porcs
s'Espardell
sa Punta d'en Talaies
Illa de sa Torreta
Cala des Bocs
s'Espalmador
s'Espardelló
es Port
Illa de s'Alga
Illa de Castaví
es Pas
es Trocadors
Platja de Llevant
Illa de Tramuntana
Illa des Pouet
Illa Rodona
Pou de ses Illetes
Salines d'en Marroig
Escull des Pou de Llevant
Punta de sa Pedrera
Caló des Moro
sa Boca
sa Roqueta
sa Punta Prima
la Savina
Ca na Costa
es Pujols
Cova de s'Aigua
Estany des Peix
Estany Pudent
Torre de sa Punta Prima
Punta des Banc
es Pujols
Punta Prima
Punta de la Gavina
es Jai Marí
Porto Saler
es Brolls
Punta Negra
Porto Saler
Sant Francesc Xavier
Sant Ferran
Cala en Baster
es Pujol des Fum
es Molins de sa Mirada
es Molí d'en Tauet
Cala en Baster
Platja de Tramuntana
Cala Saona
ses Bardetes
Camí Vell de la Mola
es Carnatge
Cingle des Cabrits
Racó de sa Creu
Punta de sa Creu
Cala Saona
Punta Rasa
ses Clotades
Caló de St. Agustí
Punta de sa Palmera
Punta Rasa
Racó Alt
Pla de ses Sitges
es Mal Pas
es Ca Marí
sa Cala
Punta des Llençol
Racó des Xiquets
ses Platgetes
es Monestir
Racó des Fonoll Marí
Racó des Caragol
Can Castelló
Castellum romà de Can Blai
Racó des Caló
Punta d'Estrips
Racó Blanc
es Mal Pas
es Arenals
es Caló
el Pilar
Racó de sa Llenya
es Corb Marí
Platja des Migjorn
es Mirador
Molí Vell de la Mola
Punta des Garroveret
Can Martí
Punta des Vell Marí
Far de la Mola
Punta de l'Anguila
la Mola
Racó de s'Alga
Mariland
Punta des Far de la Mola
es Pla del Rei
Caló des Mort
Labritja
Cala Codolar
Cap de Barbaria
Punta des Garroveret
Punta de sa Fragata
s'Estufador
Punta Roja
Cap de Barbaria